LIFE AS *Art*

Hindsight I sight Insight

GAIL MORNINGSTAR

Copyright © 2019 Gail Morningstar.
Interior Image Credit: Gail Morningstar

All rights reserved. No part of this book may be used or reproduced by any means, graphic, electronic, or mechanical, including photocopying, recording, taping or by any information storage retrieval system without the written permission of the author except in the case of brief quotations embodied in critical articles and reviews.

Balboa Press books may be ordered through booksellers or by contacting:

Balboa Press
A Division of Hay House
1663 Liberty Drive
Bloomington, IN 47403
www.balboapress.com
1 (877) 407-4847

Because of the dynamic nature of the Internet, any web addresses or links contained in this book may have changed since publication and may no longer be valid. The views expressed in this work are solely those of the author and do not necessarily reflect the views of the publisher, and the publisher hereby disclaims any responsibility for them.

Any people depicted in stock imagery provided by Getty Images are models, and such images are being used for illustrative purposes only. Certain stock imagery © Getty Images.

ISBN: 978-1-9822-2122-5 (sc)
ISBN: 978-1-9822-2123-2 (e)

Library of Congress Control Number: 2019901541

Print information available on the last page.

Balboa Press rev. date: 02/11/2019

Contents

LIFE AS ART 2

Life as Art
  The Shadow 4

LIFE AS ART 5

Life as Art
  Suffering 34

Life as Art
  Judgement 62

Life as Art
  Surrender 72

  Compassion 76

About the Author 90

Many thanks to my
Authors, Family, Friends
Clients and Colleagues
Who shared these quotes with me
Over many years

"A hundred times every day I remind myself that my inner and outer life depends on the labours of other men, living and dead, and that I must exert myself in order to give in the measure as I have received and am still receiving."
Albert Einstein

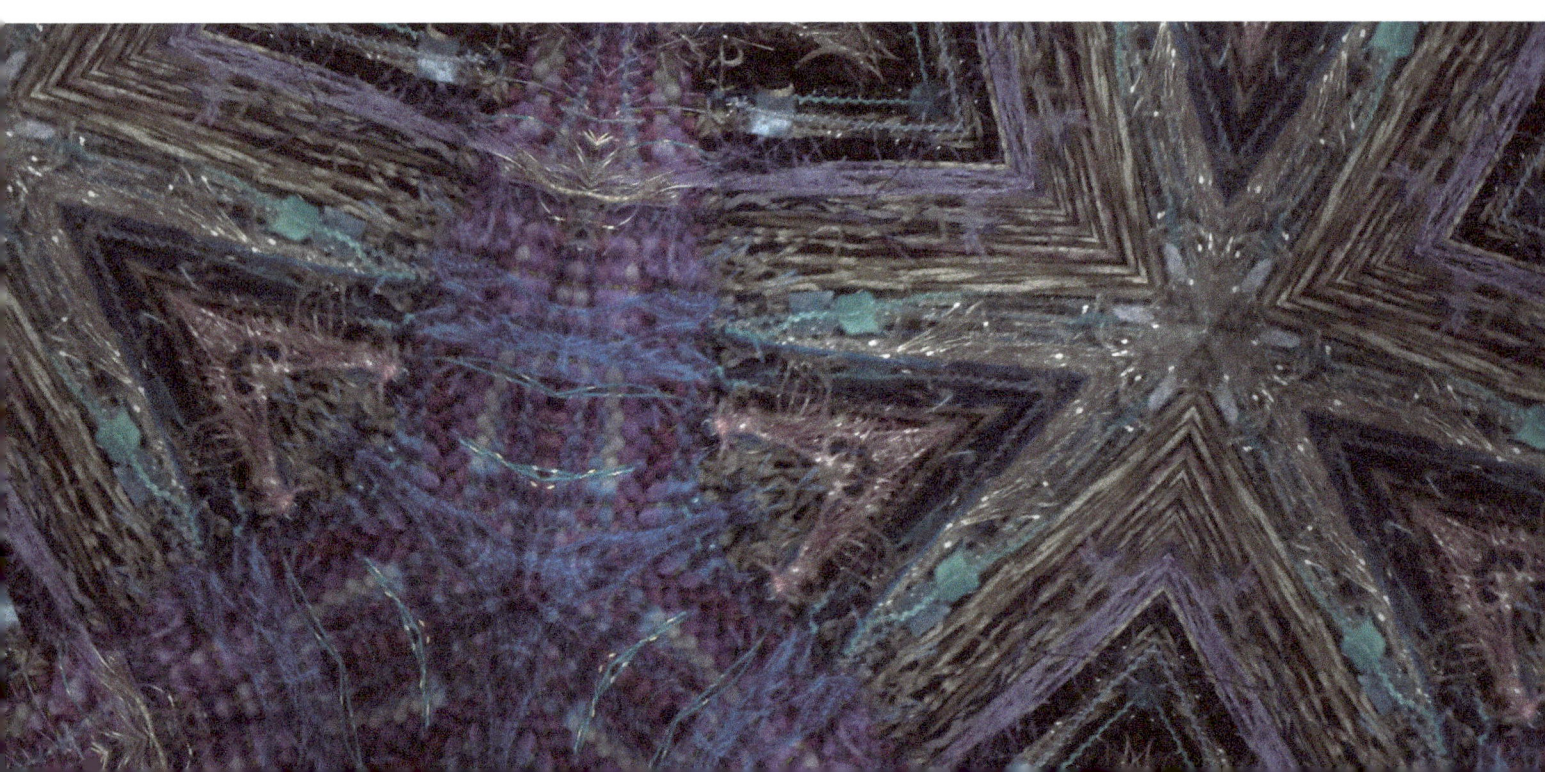

FACTS remain the same
THOUGHTS can be changed
FEELINGS change with thoughts

Try listening to your favourite music. Have a scent you enjoy close by, some water or beverage of choice, and shut off the rotation on tablet so you can look at the pictures from many perspectives. Play with the images as you would a Rorschach game. Lighting variations, mood and energy also make this journey interesting and new. The aim is joy and maybe insight.

LIFE AS ART

Hindsight   *I sight*   *Insight*

The photos in this ebook were taken from my journey using Art Therapy and Mindfulness, and are predominately from my woven wallhangings (thinking) and crocheted "Warm Hugs" (mindful meditations). I stumbled upon the kaleidoscope and other effects while exploring my new IPAD. My story is not important enough to encourage you to read this anthology, however your story is central to the journey. Think of it as a personal Rorschach game.

How do we become introspective enough to stop blaming and shaming ourselves and others? Where does the self stop and the other begin? Is blame and shame scapegoating? Is Gil Bailey correct in his assertion that scapegoating is the root of violence? Does stereotyping set the stage for Us and Them, creating the illusion of difference? The quintessential question is… Does the journey begin at the end in retrospect or self awareness before speech and action? How do we become more insightful, and learn to tolerate our shadow so we enhance our ability to be self realized?

The Beatles wrote, "All you need is love." Well, love hurts sometimes. By the same artists, "I used to be cruel to my woman I beat her and kept her apart from the things that she loved. Man I was mean but I'm changing my scene and I'm doing the best that I can. I've got to admit it's getting better a little better all the time. It can't get no worse". I-sight.

Sgt.Pepper's Lonely Hearts Club Band

Insecurity and or fear of abandonment have been sited as causes for violence. Pema Chodron wrote wonderful books on compassion; loving kindness; and becoming comfortable with uncertainty. Tara Brach and Jack Kornfield speak to the same subjects including mindful awareness. Brene Brown is essential reading on shame and vulnerability. I recommend the reader visit Hay House and Sounds True for podcasts and Ted Talks for innovative presentations.

Is compassion love or is it more complex than that? Compassion is an element of love, however, there are many variables that begin with the self. Hindsight can and often does illuminate the way if we are brave enough to look at our shadow parts. Now I assert that insight moved the Beatles toward change just as I am certain the audience will also be moved.

Blaming and shaming self and others is scapegoating. As Gil Bailey's book asserts, it is "Violence Unveiled". That is not to say we blame the victim, we put the sword down and observe the part, our shadow, that is participating in the circumstance.

Why does the person stay when the circumstance is not safe? Maybe because it is safer to stay where you know the play, rather than create a new insight that is not flattering to a 'self realized' person.

Forgiveness is required; this will lead to insight about how suffering facilitates surrender, vulnerability and compassion.

Life as Art

The Shadow

"I'm a victim of circumstance" says Larry of The Three Stooges. A victim has life done TO him. Carl Jung would say victim is one of the archetypes we could explore of the four overarching archetypes: victim, prostitute, child and saboteur.

The prostitute archetype stays for the secondary gain, whatever that may be for the individual. However, if we are all connected we must all be the victim and prostitute. Difficult to blame and shame if we are all playing the same game. The return for such insight is awareness and choice.

So too the child, in all it's incarnations: wild, playful, innocent, exploring, curious, oppositional, defiant and the list goes on. Not until we have suffered do we become violent enough to blame others and become a victim, destroying our peace of mind and, as a consequence, scapegoating.

Sabotage becomes an organic outcome of not being responsible for our own actions, thoughts and real or imagined suffering. Stereotyping facilitates our rationalizing or justifying why we are the victim of circumstances. Socialization is a construct, therefore Us and Them stereotypes keep us stuck in the continuous shadow archetypal cycle of victim, prostitute, child and saboteur.

What about forgiveness; could that be the panacea? Plenty of therapies say so. Forgive who for what? If I am suffering, is it of my own volition? Do my judgements unexamined impede my journey to forgiveness, love and compassion?

LIFE AS ART

What do the great thinkers have to say about the antidote to violence and opening to compassion?

"What you can do, or dream you can do, begin it; boldness has genius, power, and magic in it."
                                                                                        Goethe

"The best day of your life is the one on which you decide life is your own. No apologies or excuses. No one to lean on, rely on or blame. The gift is yours - it is an amazing journey - and you alone are responsible for the quality of it. This is the day your life really begins."

Bob Moawad

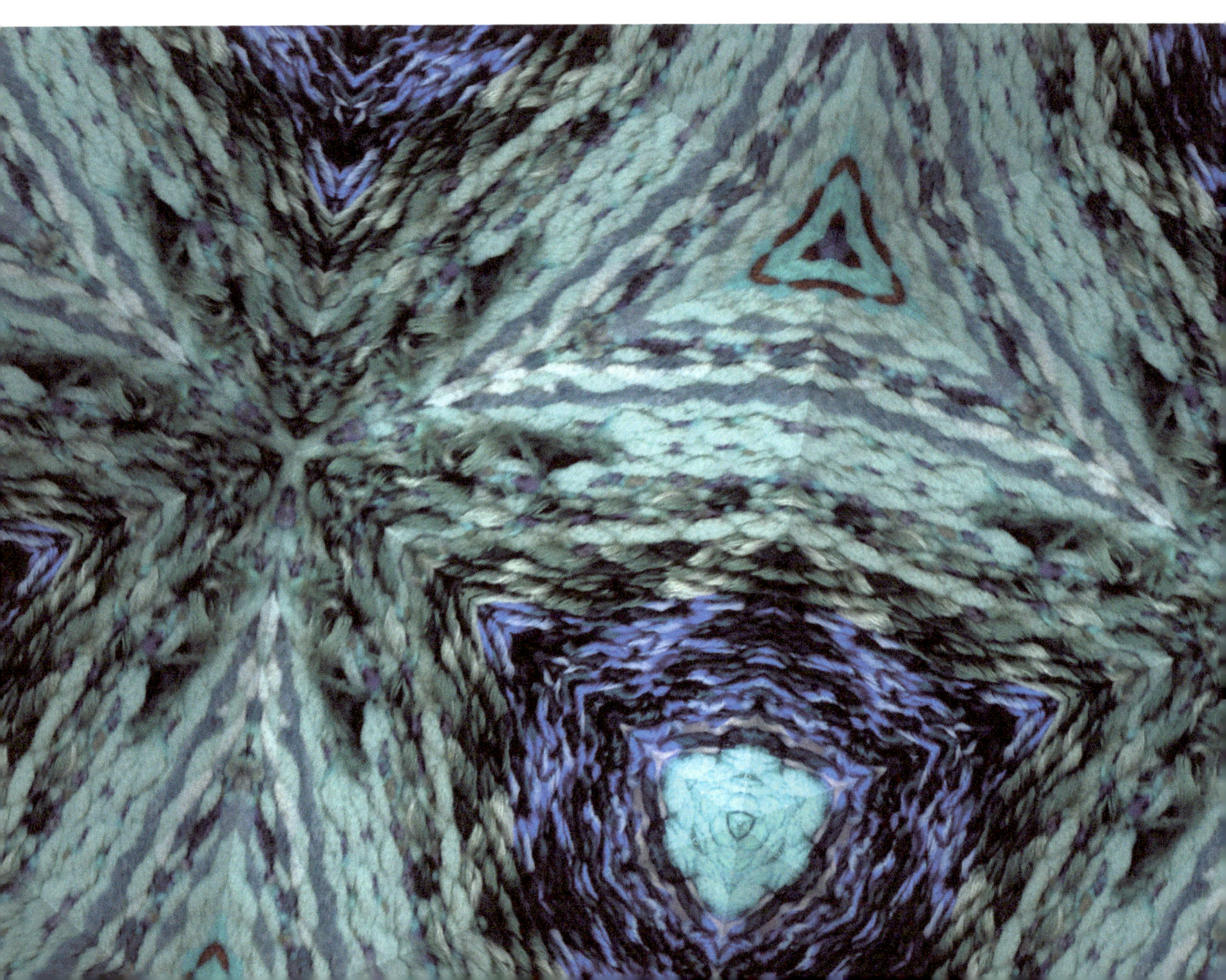

"We forge gradually our greatest instrument for understanding the world—Introspection. We discover that humanity may resemble us very considerably—that the best way of knowing the inwardness of our neighbours is to know ourselves."

Walter Lippmann

"Art is the window to a man's soul. Without it, he would never be able to see beyond his immediate world; nor could the world see the man within."

Lady Bird Johnson

"I care not so much what I am in the opinion of others, as what I am in my own; I would be rich of myself, and not by borrowing."

Michel De Montaigne

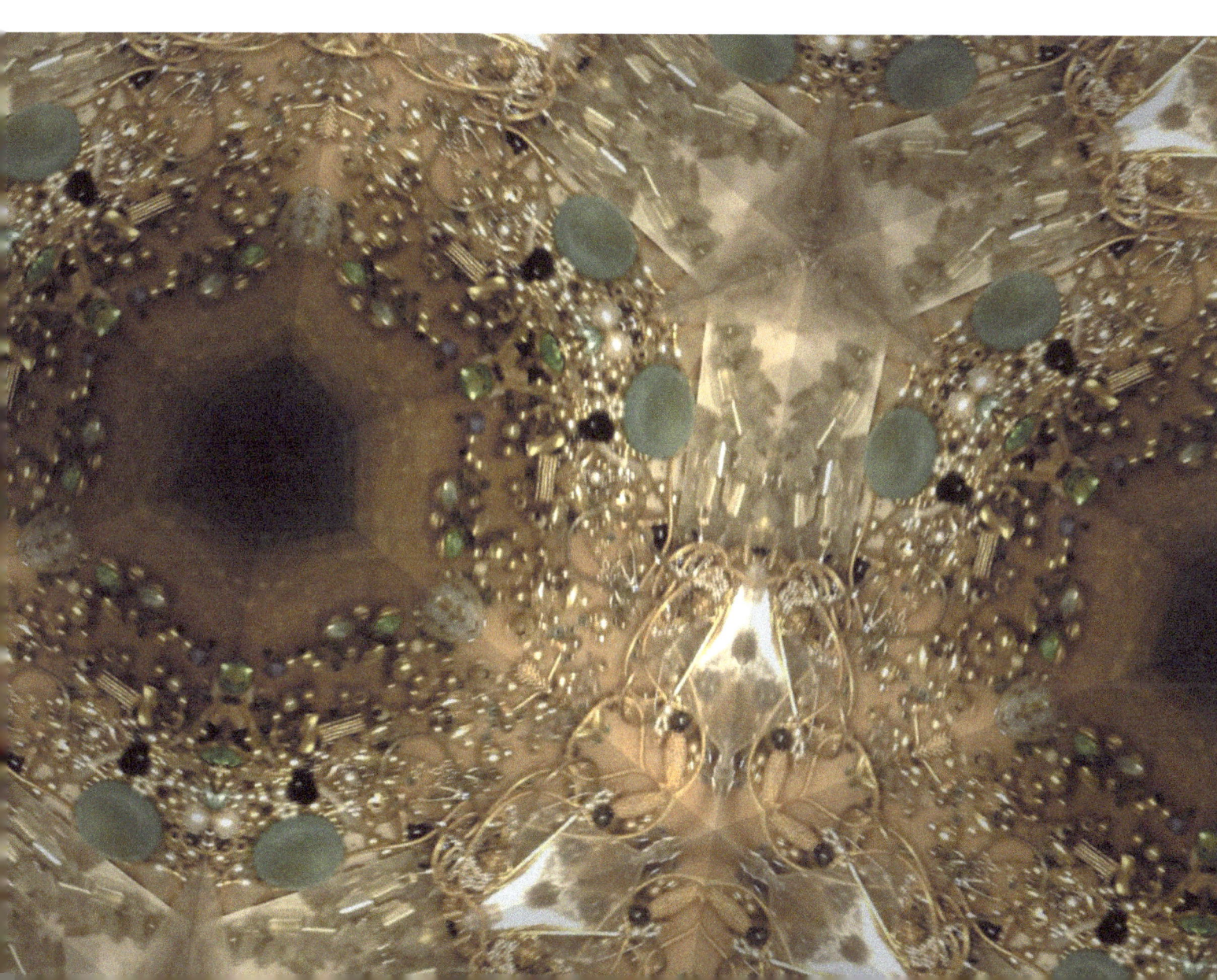

"The bees plunder the flowers here and there; but afterward they produce honey, which is peculiarly their own."

Michel De Montaigne

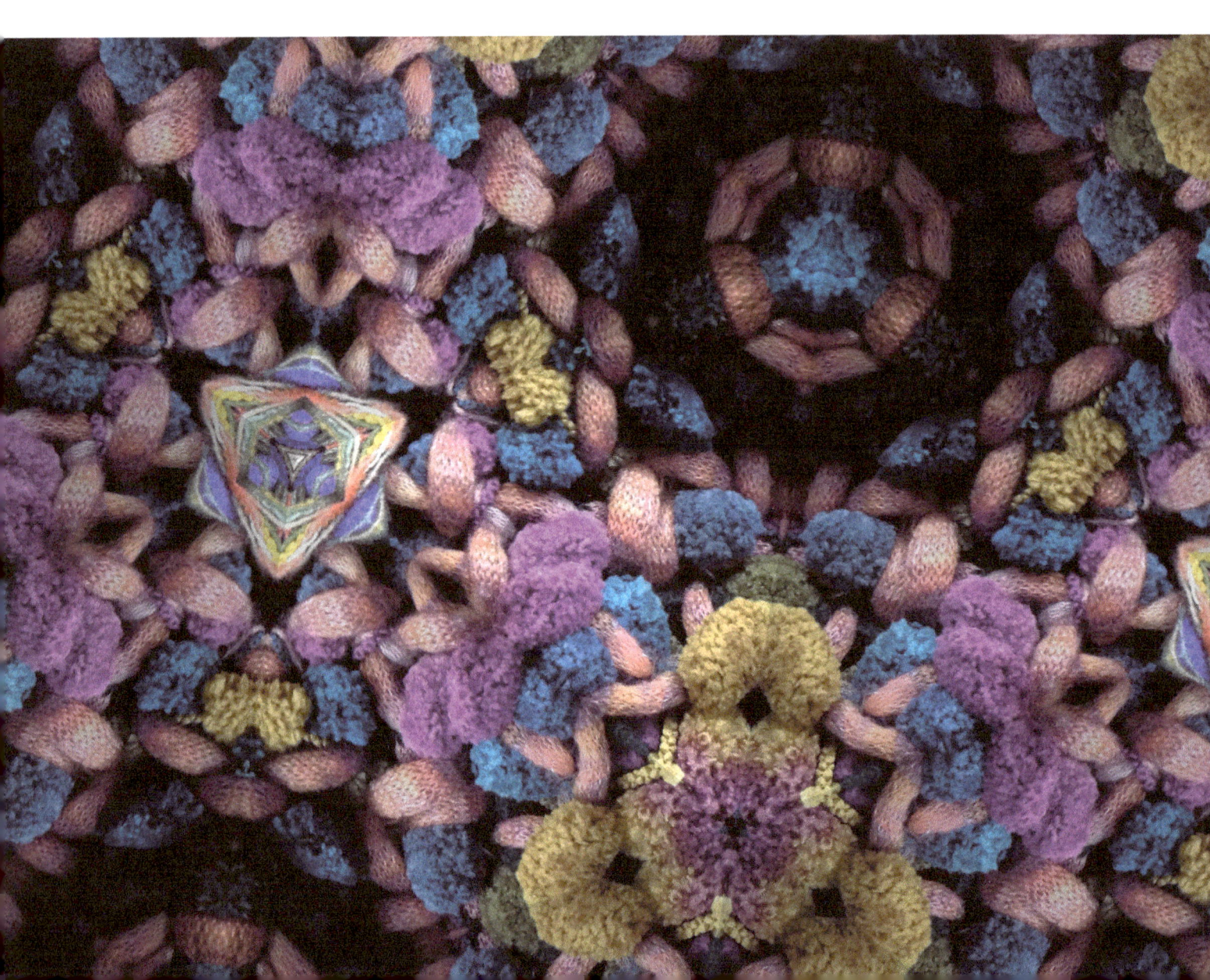

The only means of strengthening one's intellect is to make up one's mind about nothing - to let the mind be a thoroughfare for all thoughts."

John Keats

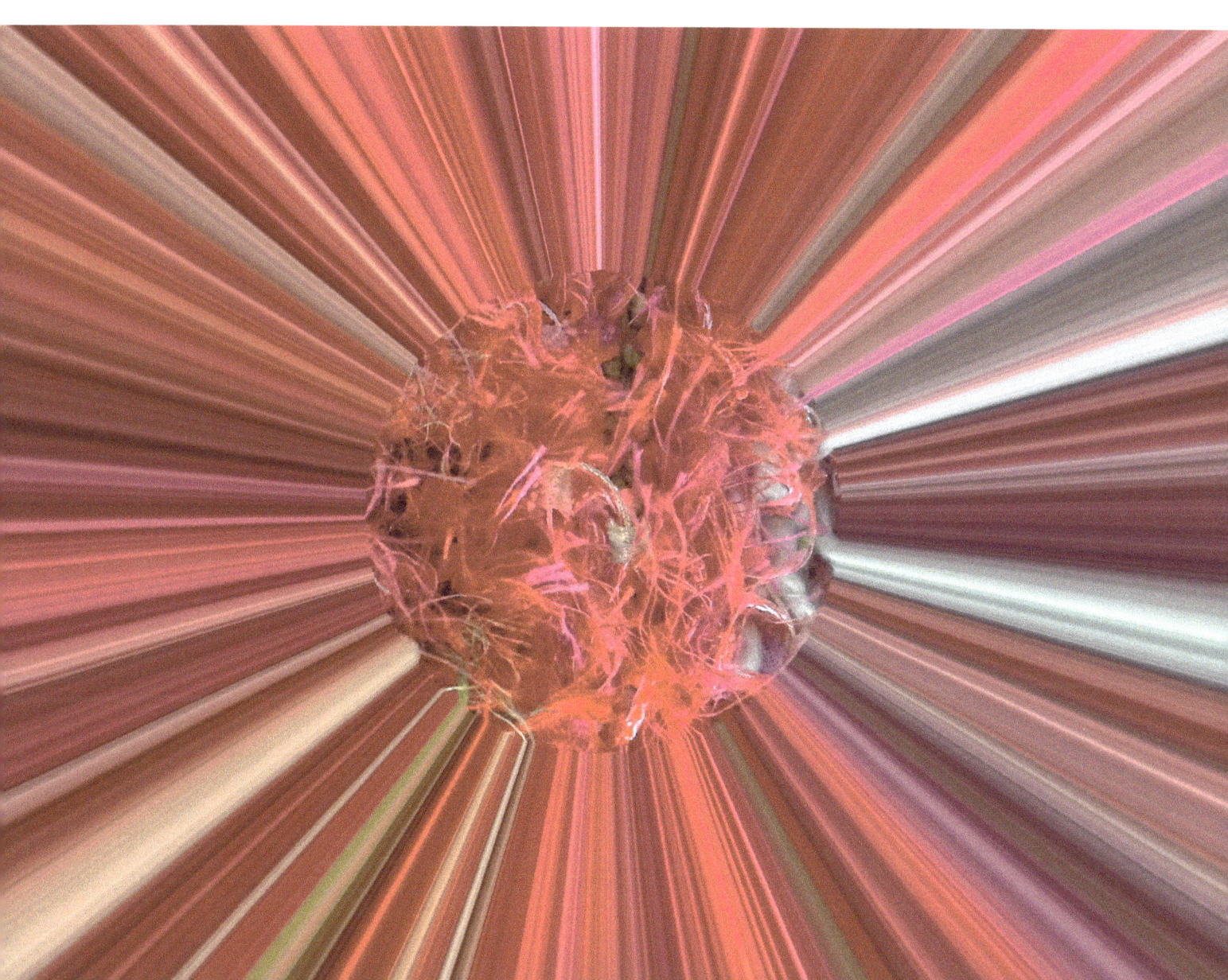

"*I love the night. I love to feel the tide of darkness rising slowly and slowly washing, turning over and over, lifting, floating, all that lies strewn upon the dark beach, all that lies hid in rocky hollows.*"

Katherine Mansfield

"Look at every path closely and deliberately. Try it as many times as you think necessary. Then ask yourself and yourself alone one question…. Does this path have a heart? If it does, the path is good. If it doesn't it is of no use."

Carlos Castenada

"Empty pockets never held anyone back. Only empty heads and hearts can do that."

Norman Vincent Peale

"Love your neighbor—He's having just as much trouble as you are."

Norman Vincent Peale

"So many people dwell on negativity, and I've survived by ignoring it: It dims your light and it's harder each time to turn the power up again."

Judith Jamison

"There is one thing alone that stands the brunt of life throughout its course: a quiet conscience."

Euripides

"Stop looking for a scapegoat in your life but be willing to face the truth within yourself and right your own wrongs."

Eileen Caddy

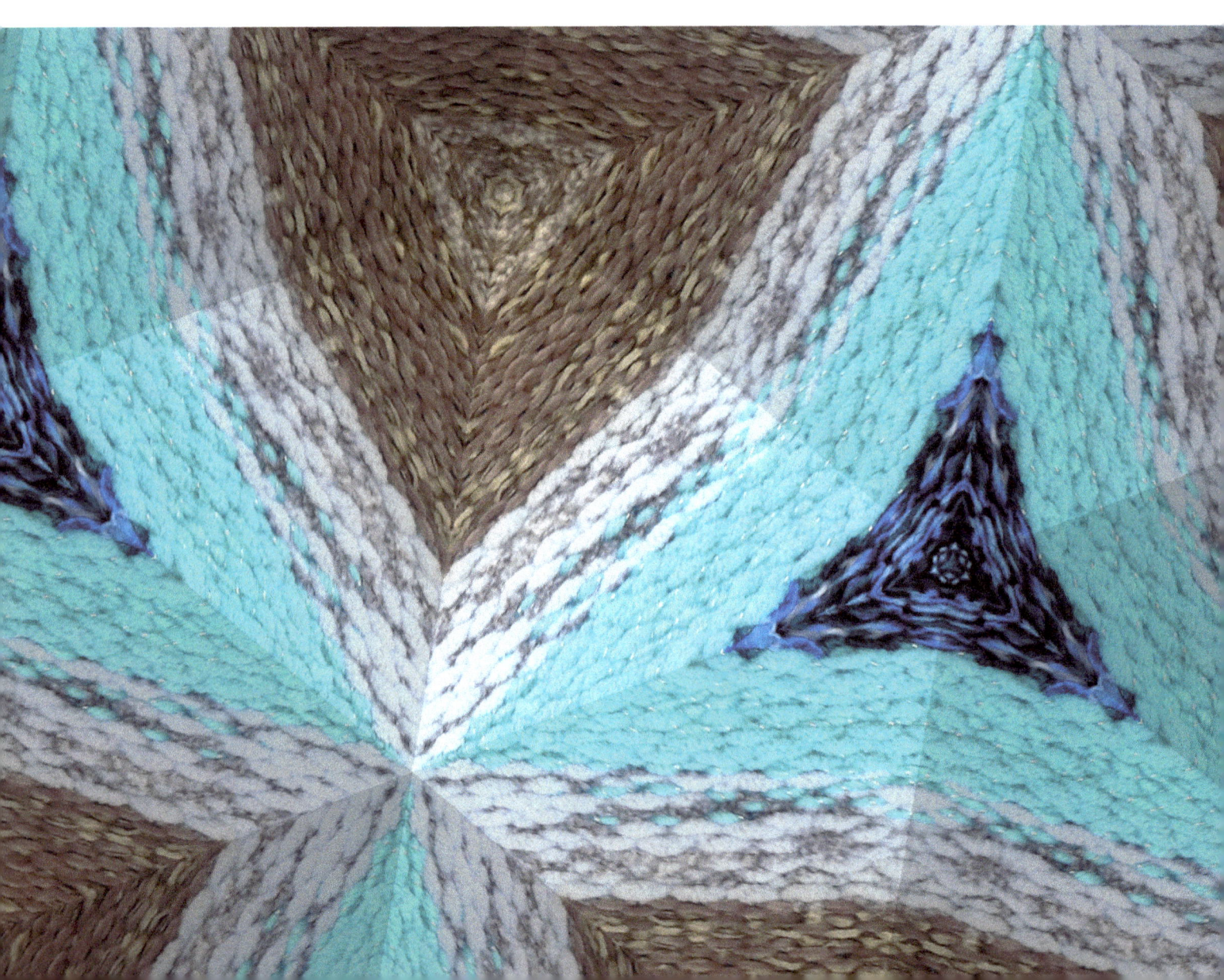

"*Time will reveal everything. It is a babbler, and speaks even when not asked.*"

Euripides

"I swore never to be silent whenever human beings endure suffering and humiliation. We must always take sides. Neutrality helps the oppressor, never the victim. Silence encourages the tormentor, never the tormented"

Elie Wiesel

"There are two big forces at work, external and internal. We have very little control over external forces such as tornadoes, earthquakes, floods, disasters, illness and pain. What really matters is the internal force. How do I respond to those disasters? Over that I have complete control."

Leo Bascaglia

"The wise learn from the experience of others, and the creative know how to make a crumb of experience go a long way."

Eric Hoffer

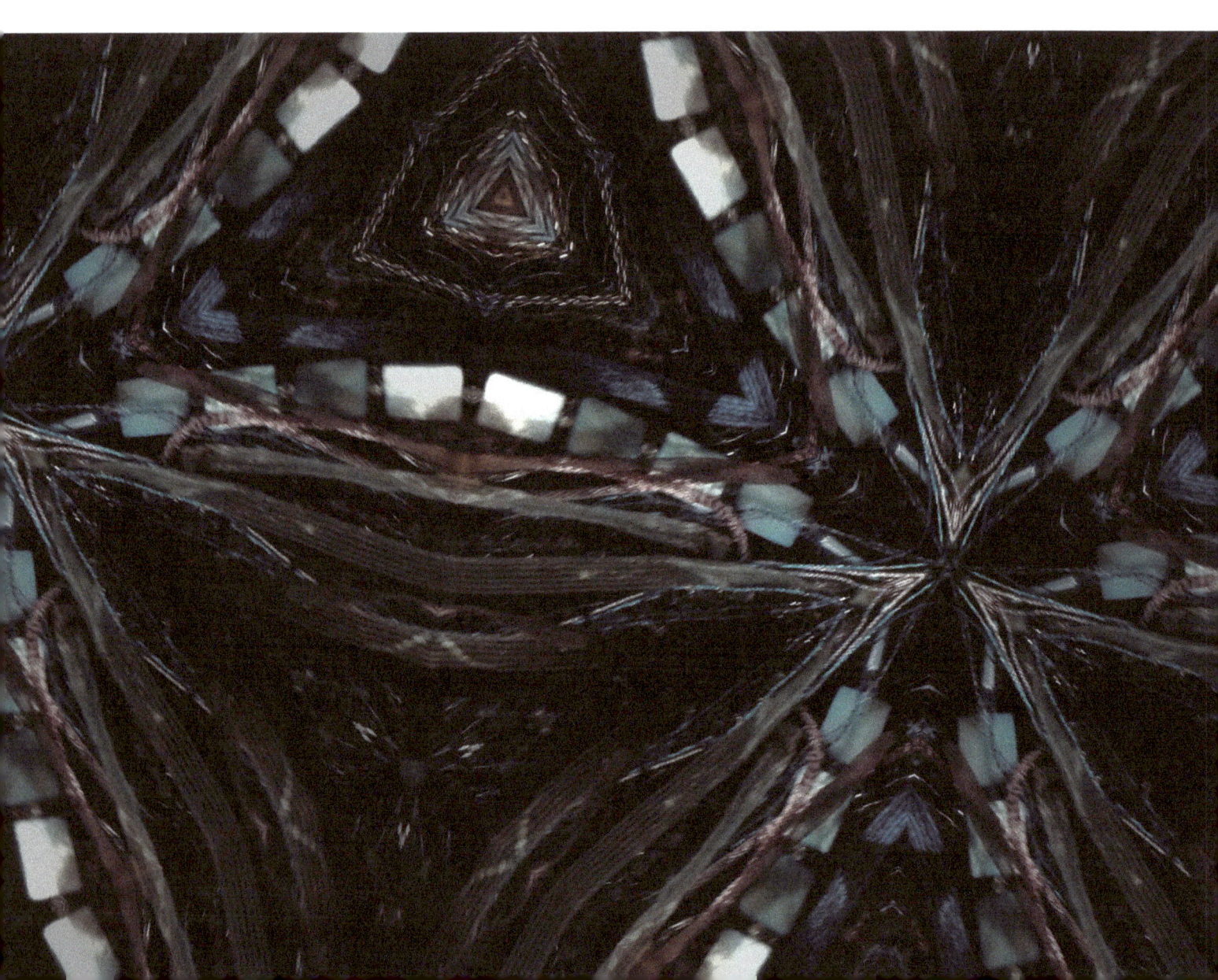

"It is true that we shall not be able to reach perfection, but on our struggle toward it we shall strengthen our characters and give stability to our ideas, so that, whilst ever advancing calmly in the same direction, we shall be rendered capable of applying the faculties with which we have been gifted to the best possible account."

Confucius

"I do not sit down at my desk to put into verse something that is already clear in my mind. If it were clear in my mind, I should have no incentive or need to write about it. We do not write in order to be understood; We write in order to understand."

C. Day Lewis

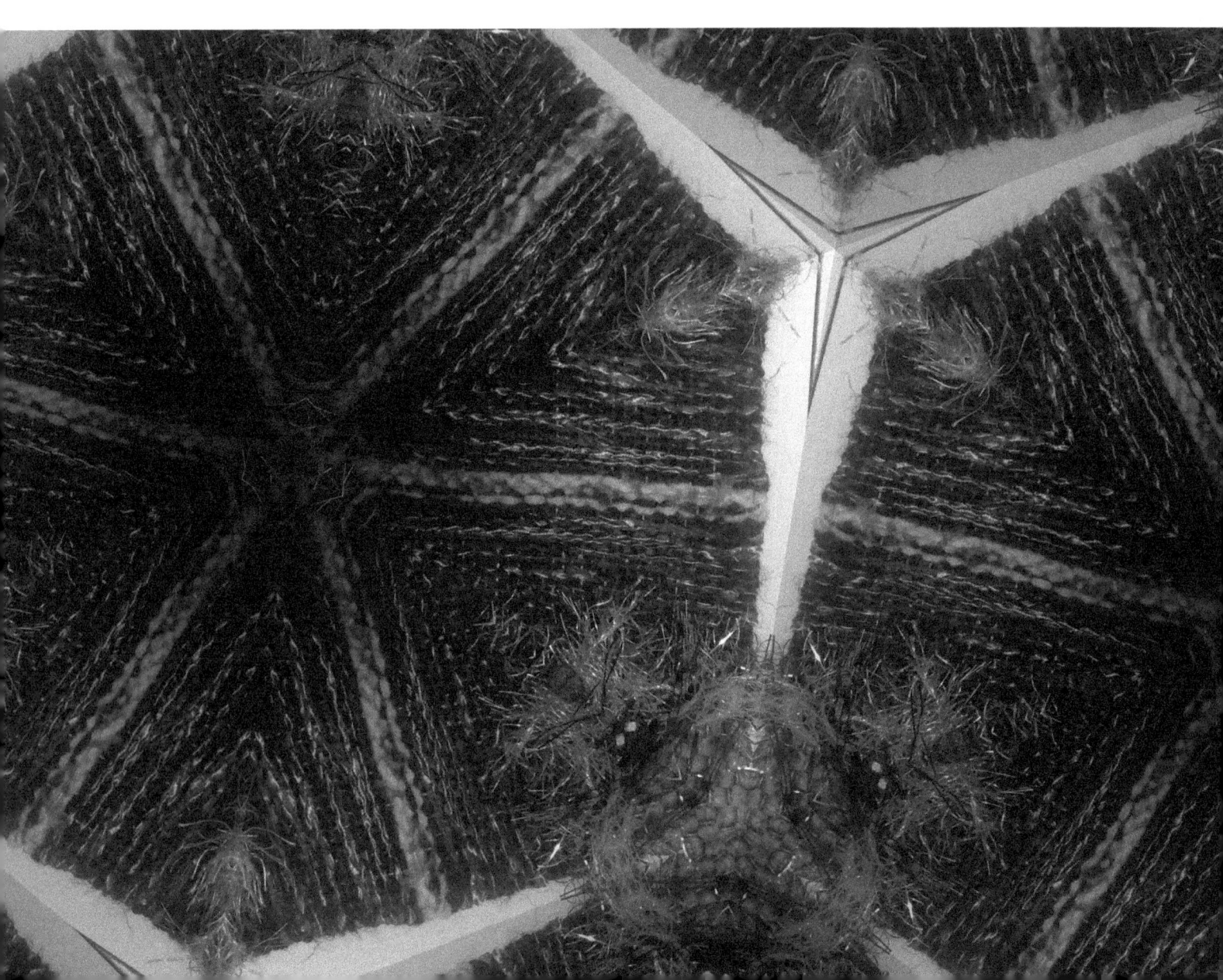

"A poem begins as a lump in the throat, a sense of wrong, a homesickness, a lovesickness. It finds the thought and the thought finds the words."

Robert Frost

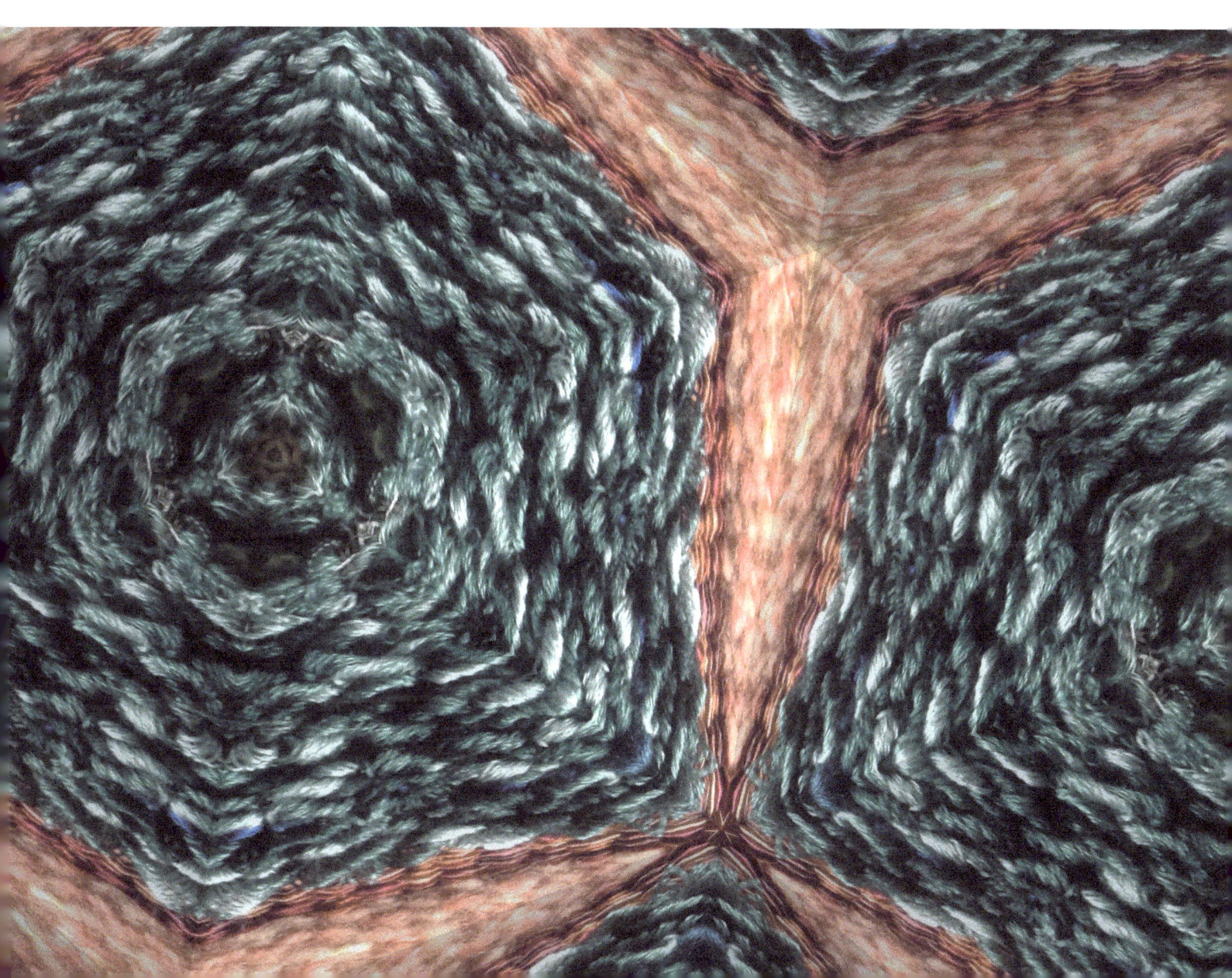

"Poetry is what gets lost in translation.

Robert Frost

"The best way out is through"

Robert Frost

"If a friend is in trouble, don't annoy him by asking if there is anything you can do. Think up something appropriate and do it."

Edgar Watson Howe

"*I believe that everything happens for a reason. People change so that you can learn to let go, things go wrong so that you appreciate them when they're right, you believe lies so you eventually learn to trust no one but yourself, and sometimes good things fall apart so better things can fall together.*"

Marilyn Monroe

"It may be hard for an egg to turn into a bird: It would be a jolly sight harder for it to learn to fly while remaining an egg. We are like eggs at present. And you cannot go on indefinitely being just an ordinary, decent egg. We must be hatched or go bad."

C.S. Lewis

"Speak when you are angry - and you will make the best speech you'll ever regret."

Laurence J. Peters

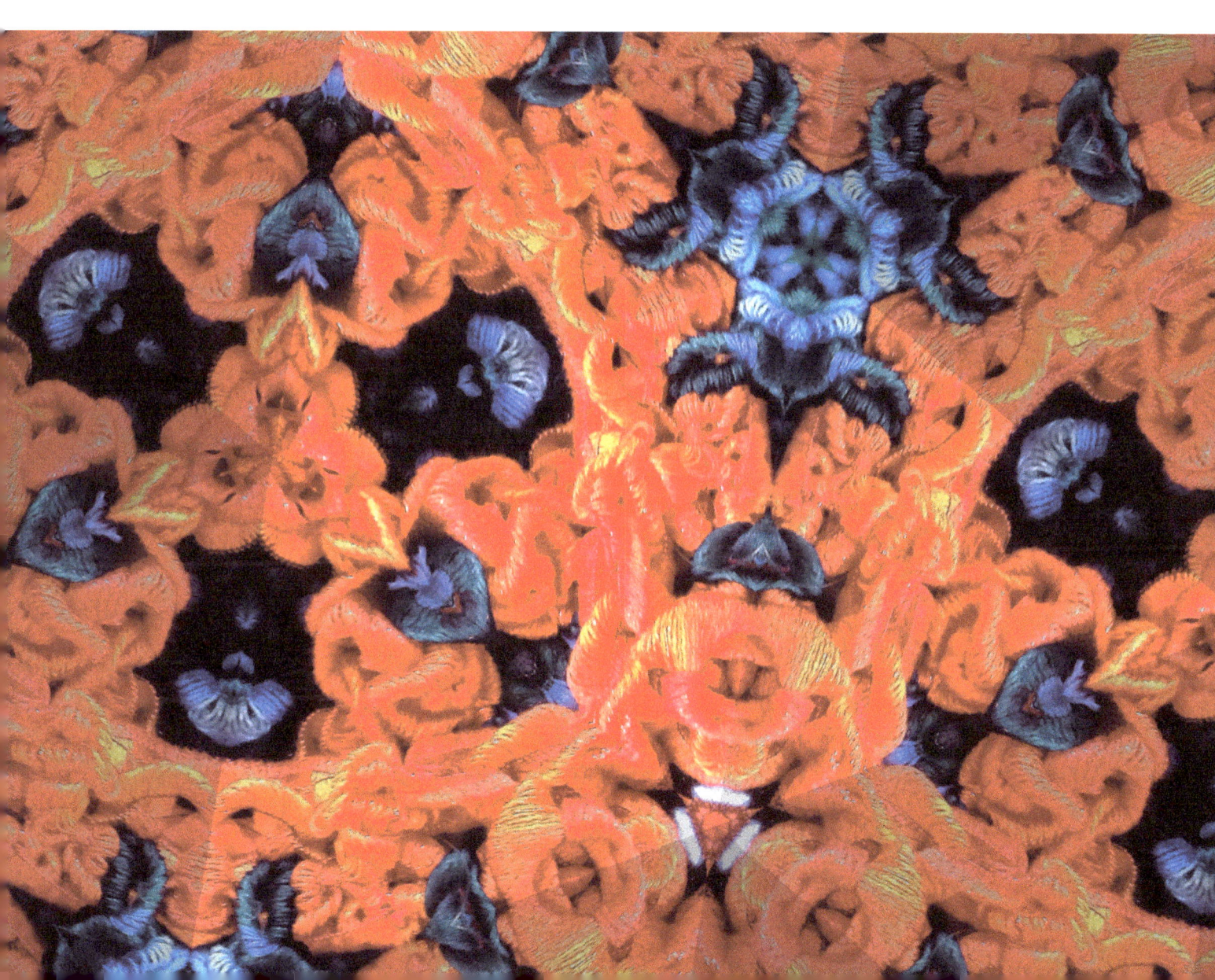

"The work, my friend is peace. More than an end of this war - an end to the beginnings of all wars."

Franklin D. Roosevelt

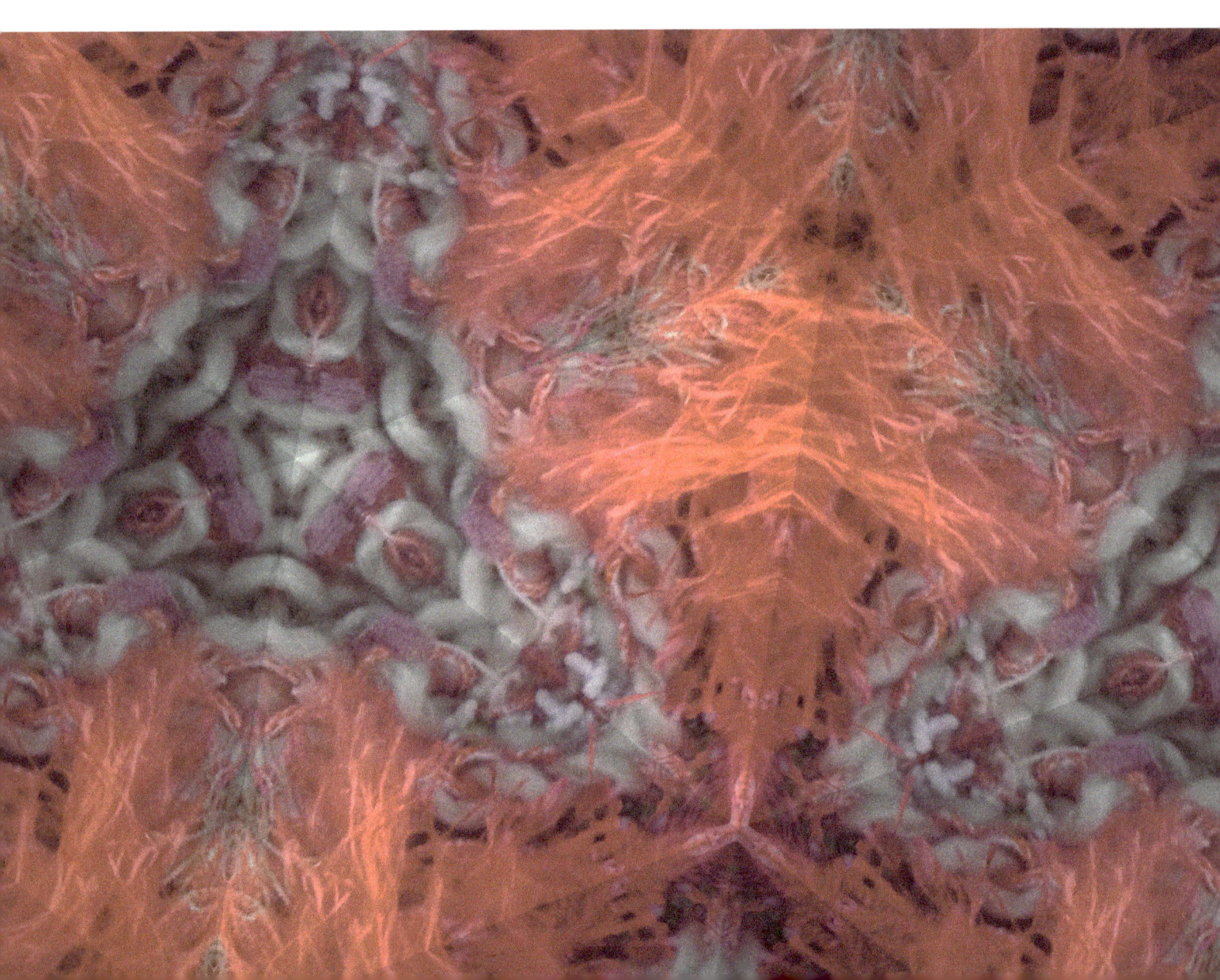

"Embracing your shame is paradoxically what heals it"

Raphael Cushnir

Life as Art

Suffering

The first Noble Truth: Life is suffering. We are supposed to know that loss of a loved one creates suffering and the depth of love equals the depth of suffering. Should we love less so we suffer less; do we have a choice?

Tom Waits said, "I'd rather have a bottle in front of me than a frontal lobotomy"; pick your poison, only to ruin the liver and postpone the inevitable introspection about culpability; to examine the source and defend or dismiss, after discernment.

"Warriorship is a continual journey. To be a warrior is to learn to be genuine in every moment of your life."
Chogyam Trungpa

"Suffering is meaningful. Suffering can be endured because there is a reason for it that is worth the effort."
Gary Zukav

"We are made up of our past experiences - hurts, pleasures, fears, losses and gains. We are a composite of the past. The self is intricately woven into this fabric of past experiences and responses, and it requires the continued existence of the past in order to continue it's own existence…We never meet life anew"

John McAfee

"It is by suffering that human beings become angels."

Victor Hugo

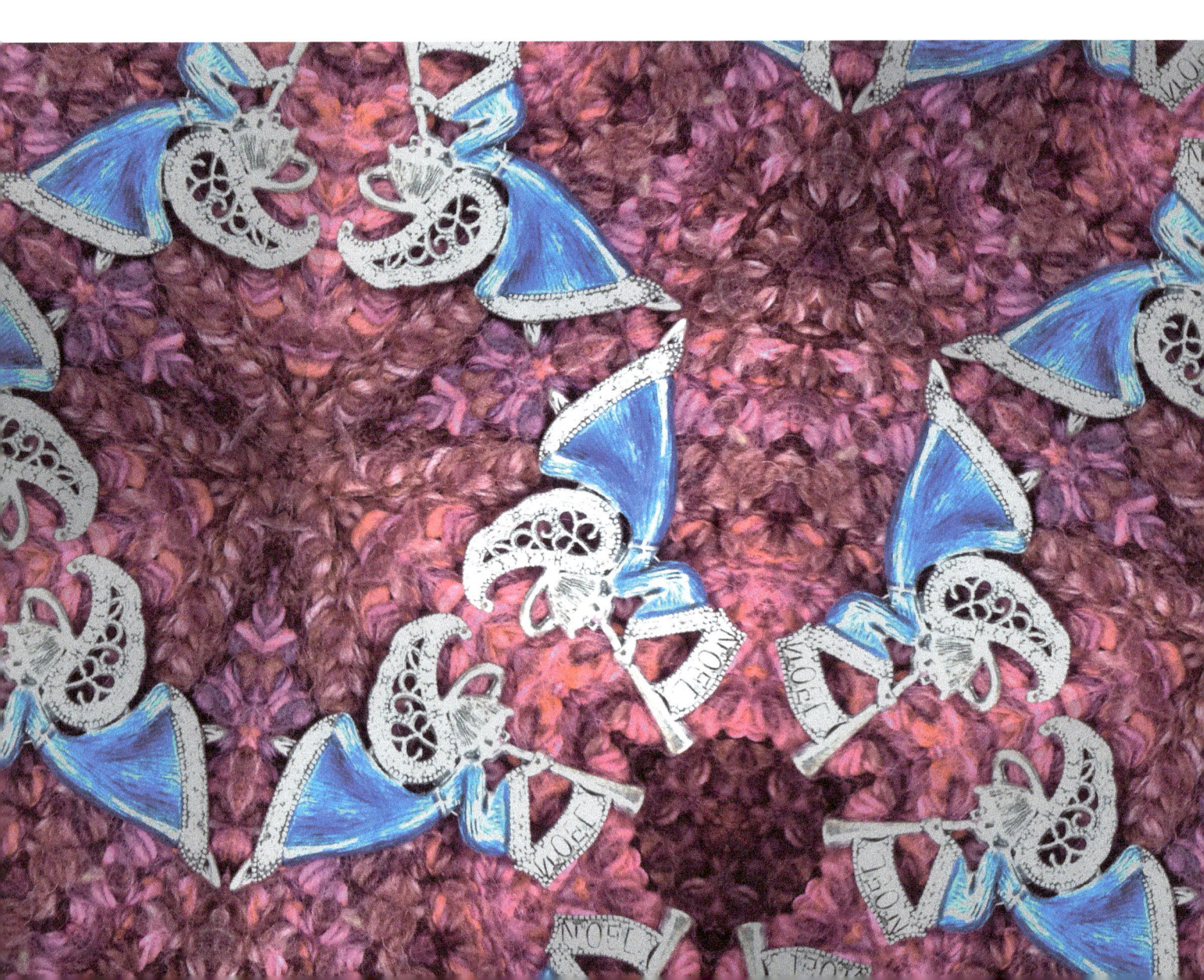

"Do not finish your work too much. An impression is not sufficiently durable for its first freshness to survive a belated search for infinite detail."

Paul Gauguin

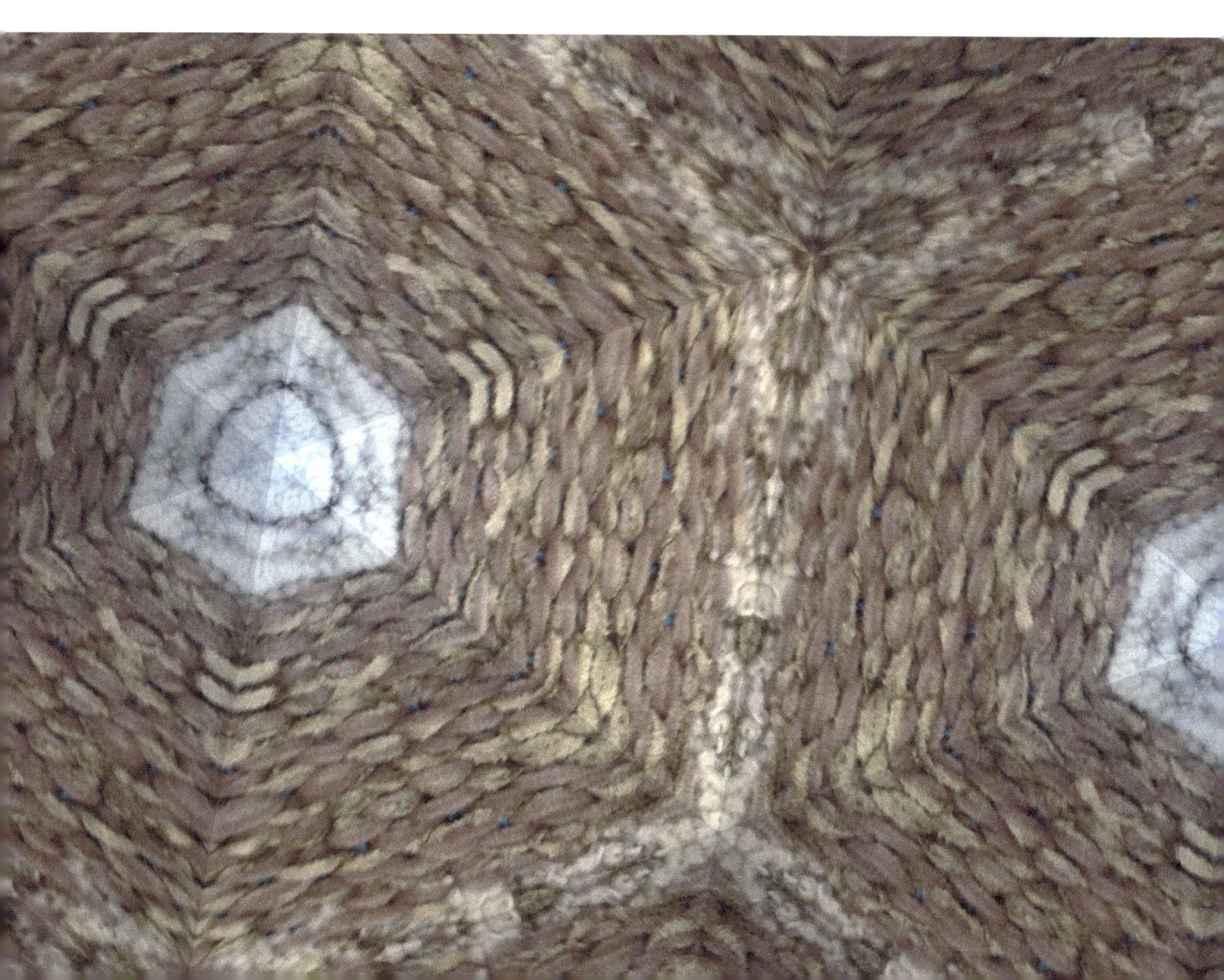

"Life is not what is said, but the process of saying, not the created picture, but the creating."

Gerhard Richter

"In order to create there must be a dynamic force, and what force is more potent than love?"

Igor Stravinsky

"Shall I tell you what I think are the two qualities of a work of art? First, it must be the indescribable, and second, it must be inimitable."

Pierre Augustuste Renior

"MY dear Tristan, to be an artist at all is like living in Switzerland during a world war."

Tom Stoppard

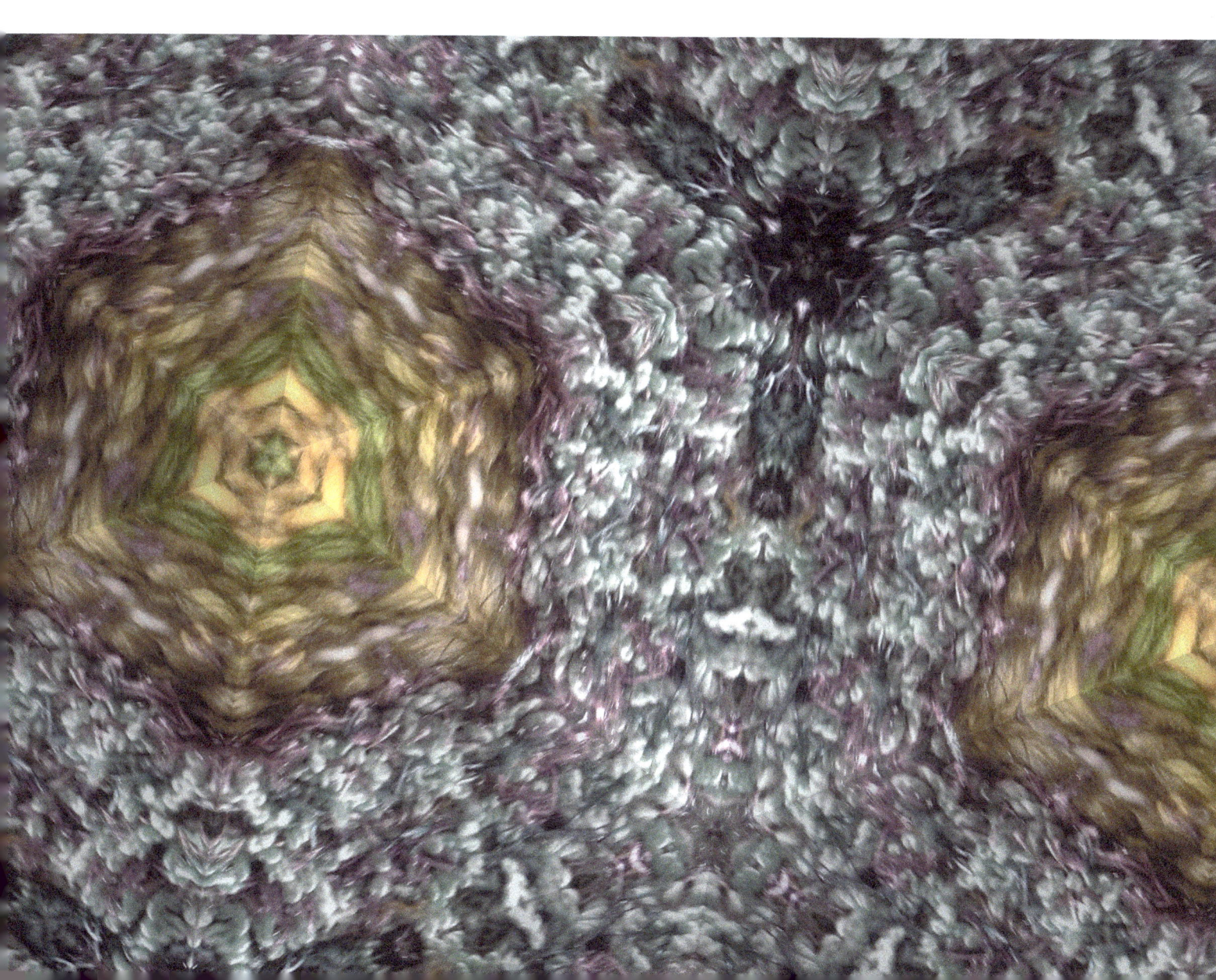

"Art advances between two chasms, which are frivolity and propaganda. On the ridge where the great artist moves forward, every step is an adventure, an extreme risk. In that risk, however, and only there, lies the freedom of art."

Albert Camus

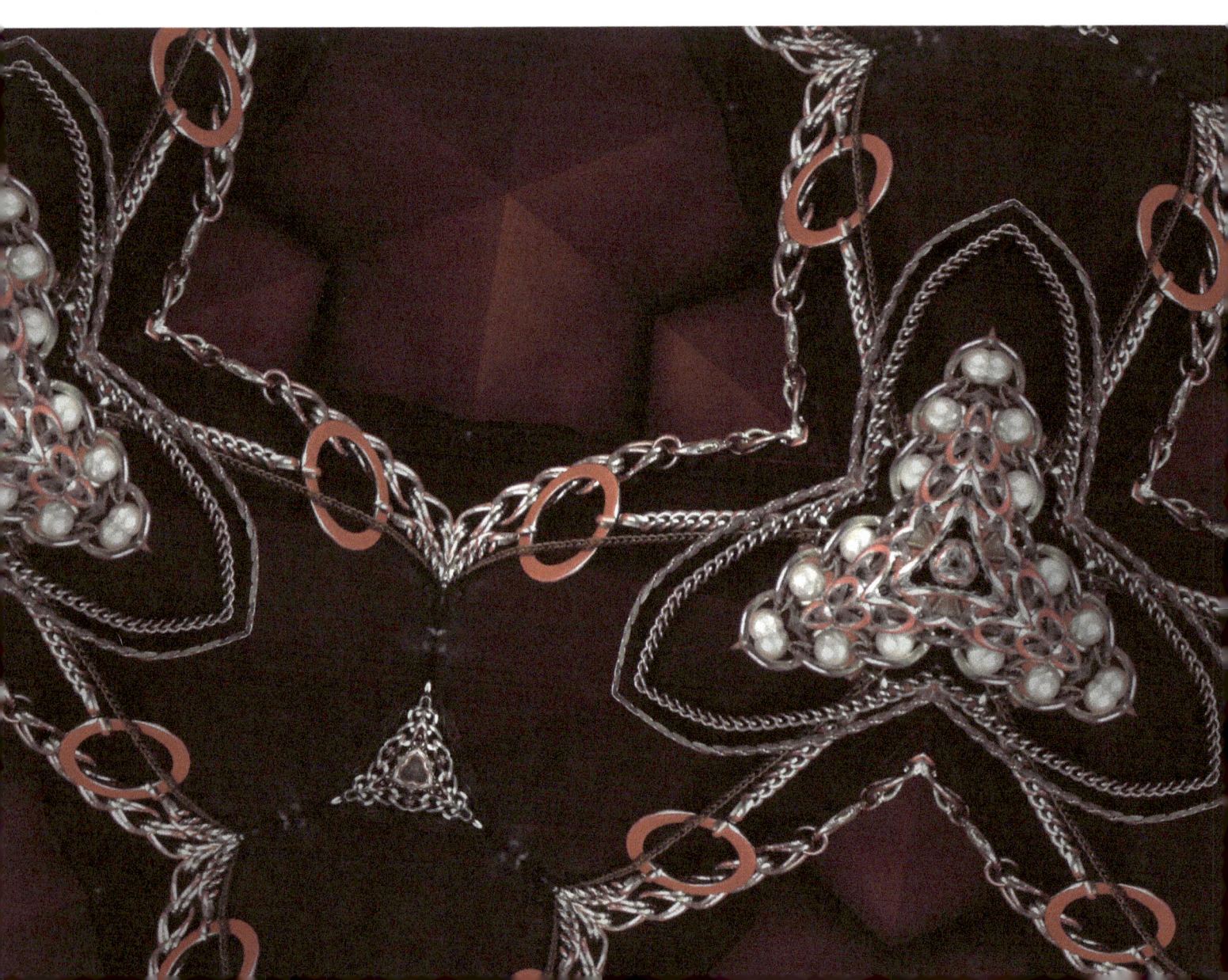

"Art is a lie that makes us realize the truth."

Pablo Picasso

"Artists to my mind are the real architects of change, and not the political legislators who implement change after the fact."

William S. Burroughs

"I suppose I am basically a clerk, a cataloguer. I like the reductiveness of that, I like the stripping down, the basic form of organization."

Peter Greenway

"Openness doesn't come from resisting our fears but rather from getting to know them well."

Pema Chodron

"Reality is that which, when you stop believing in it, doesn't go away."

Philip K. Dick

"We delight in the beauty of the butterfly, but rarely admit the changes it has gone through to achieve that beauty."

Maya Angelou

"Let the fear of a danger be a spur to prevent it: he that fears not, gives advantage to the danger."

Francis Quarrel

"For me, a landscape does not exist in its own right, since its appearances changes every moment."

Claude Monet

'I must create a system Or be enslaved by another man's; I will not reason or compare; my business is to create."

William Blake

"Art is wonderfully irrational, exuberantly pointless, but necessary all the same."

Gunter Grass

"Or the waterfall, or music heard so deeply
That it is not heard at all, but you are the music
While the music lasts. These are only hints and guesses,
Hints followed by guesses; and the rest Is prayer, observance, discipline, thought and action. The hint half guessed, the gift half understood, is Incarnation.

                                                                                                                T. S. Eliot

"They teach you there's a boundary line to music. But man, there's no boundary line to art."

Charley Parker

"But sorrow, gladness, yearning, hope, love belonging to all of us, in all times and in all places. Music is the only means whereby we feel these emotions in their universality."

H.A. Overstreet

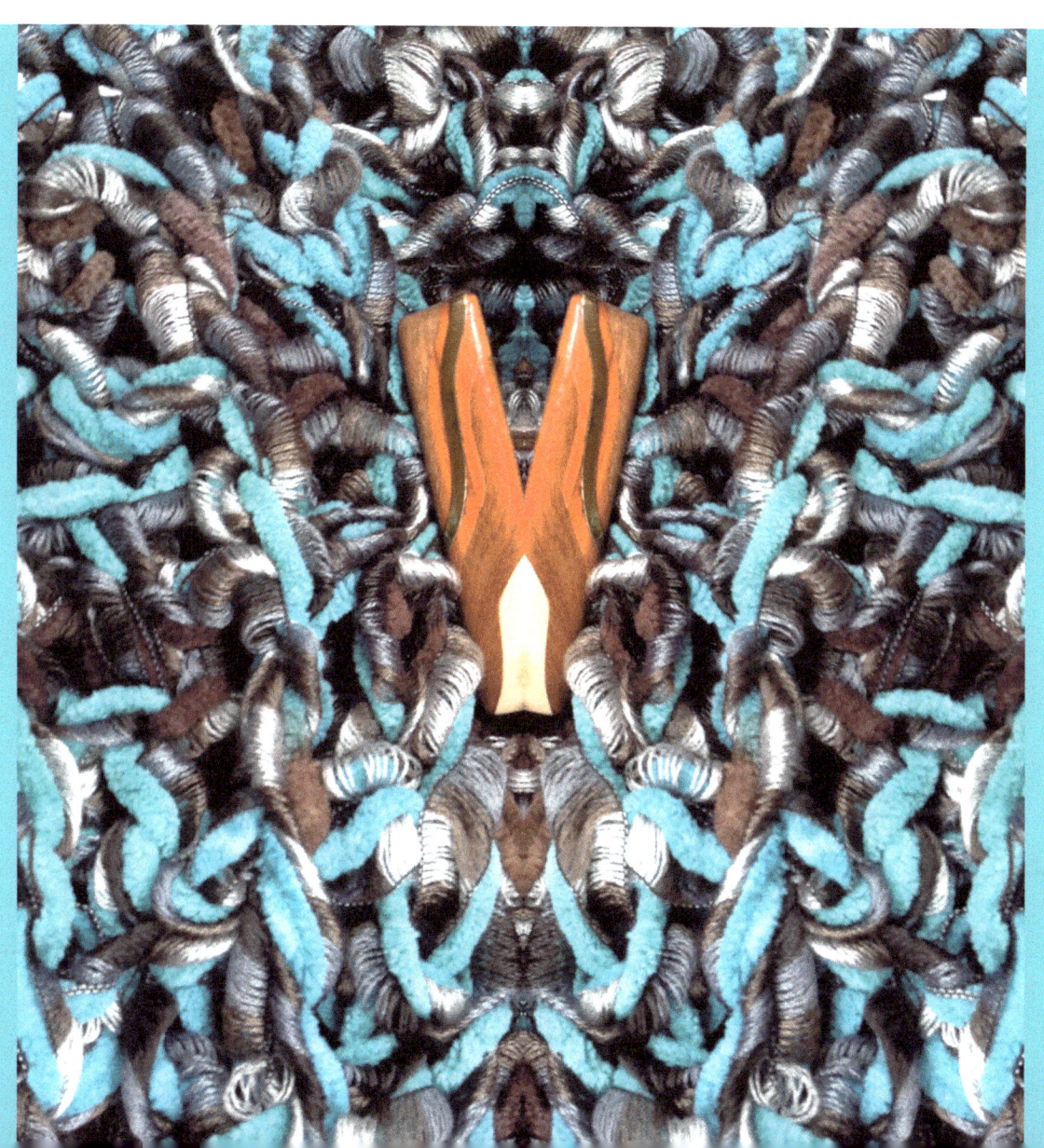

"The mind is a strange machine which can combine the materials offered to it in the most astonishing ways."

Bertrand Russell

"There are two means of refuge from the miseries of life: music and cats."

Schweitzer

"I know this, with sure and certain knowledge: a man's work is nothing but this slow trek to rediscover, through the detours of art, those two or three great and simple images in whose presence his heart first opened."

Albert Camus

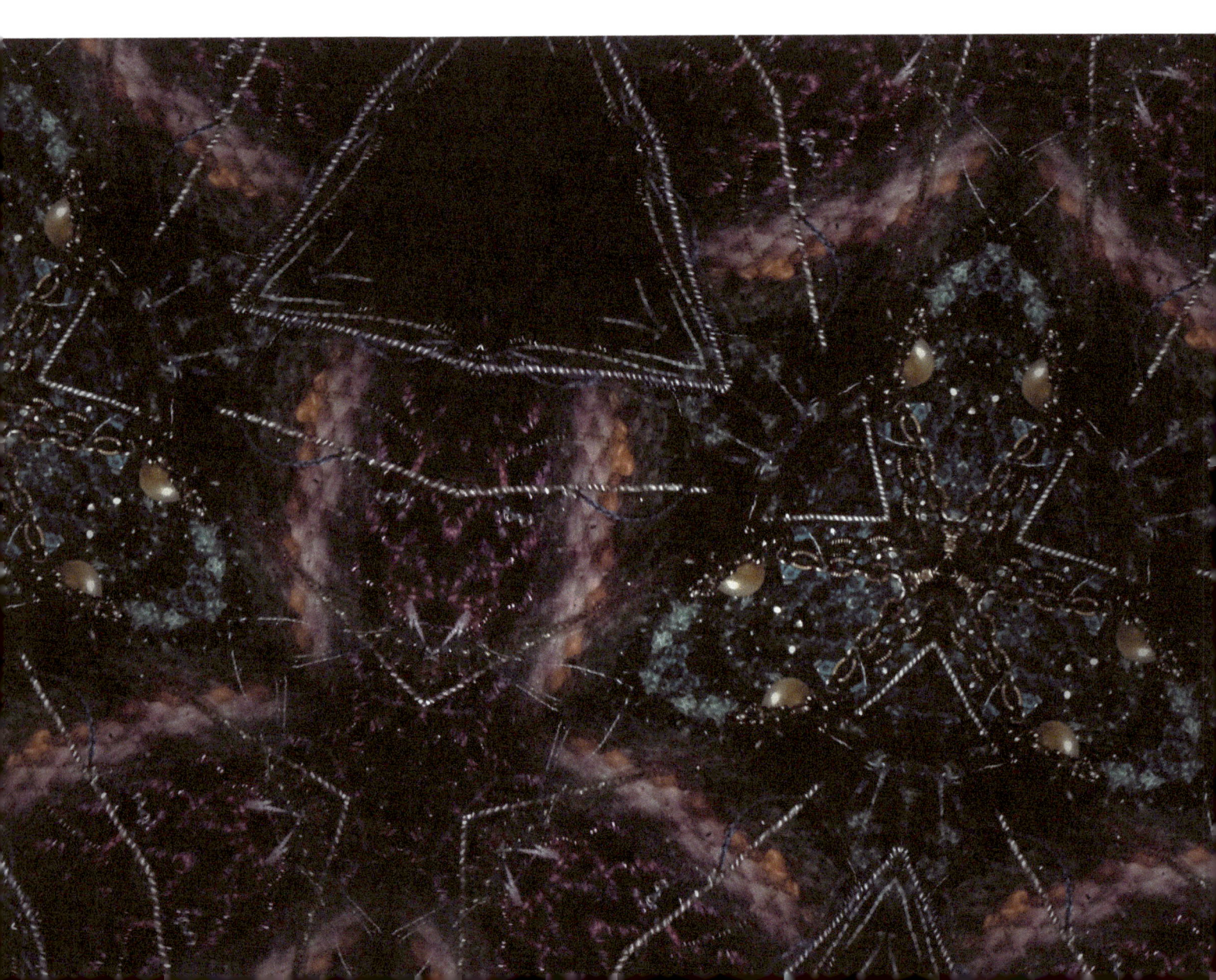

"*Any great work of art… revives and readapts time and space and the measure of its success is the extent of which it makes you an inhabitant of that world - the extent to which it invites you in and lets you breath its strange, special air.*"

Leonard Bernstein

"Colors are the smiles of nature. When they are extremely smiling, and break forth into other beauty besides, they are her laughs as in the flowers."

Leigh Hunt

"The Romans would never have found time to conquer the world if they had been obliged to learn Latin."

Heinrich Heine

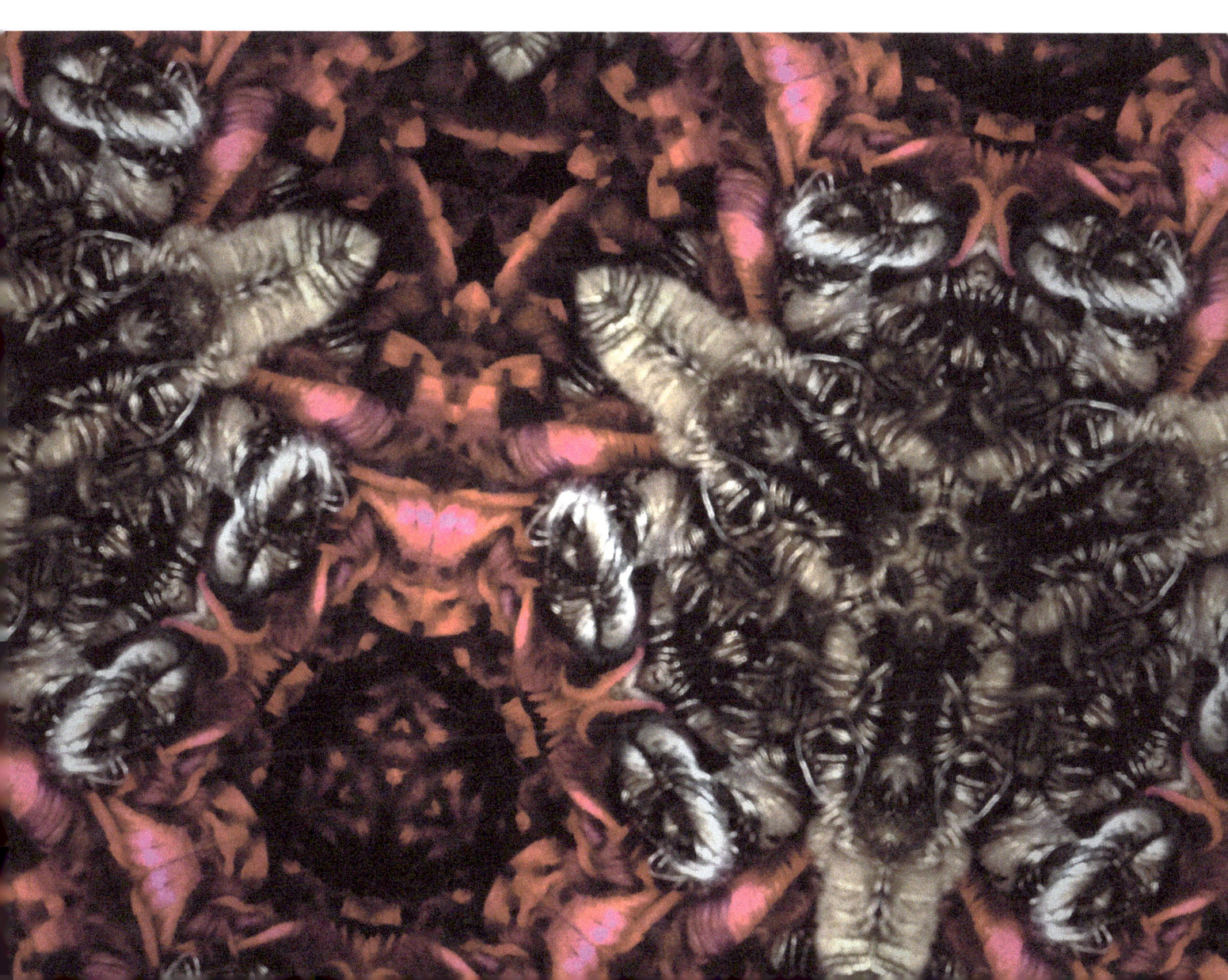

Life as Art

Judgement

Judgements unobserved become the breeding ground of Us and Them. As I reflect on my judgements, I become aware of the neutrality necessary to begin forgiveness. Many judgements are opinions or personal values. It becomes invaluable to be discerning about what is mine and what belongs to someone else. There are Social Norms that help us get along and live by the rules of our particular culture; but what about inclusion? Often our slights are confusion of a cultural difference. However, shaming someone for their difference only victimizes them and puts the blame on us for our ignorance. Violence could ensue if we are not mindful. Indeed, finding the courage to ask questions and to clarify the situation, can avoid many misunderstandings.

"Everybody is a genius. But if you judge a fish by its ability to climb a tree, it will live its whole life believing it is stupid."

Albert Einstein

"The paradox of reality is that no image is as compelling as the one which exists in the mind's eye."

Shana Alexander

"Life is simply time given to man to learn how to live. Mistakes are always part of learning. The real dignity of life consists in cultivating a fine attitude towards our own mistakes and those of the others."

William Jordan

"In order to live free and happily you must sacrifice boredom. It is not always an easy sacrifice."

Richard Bach

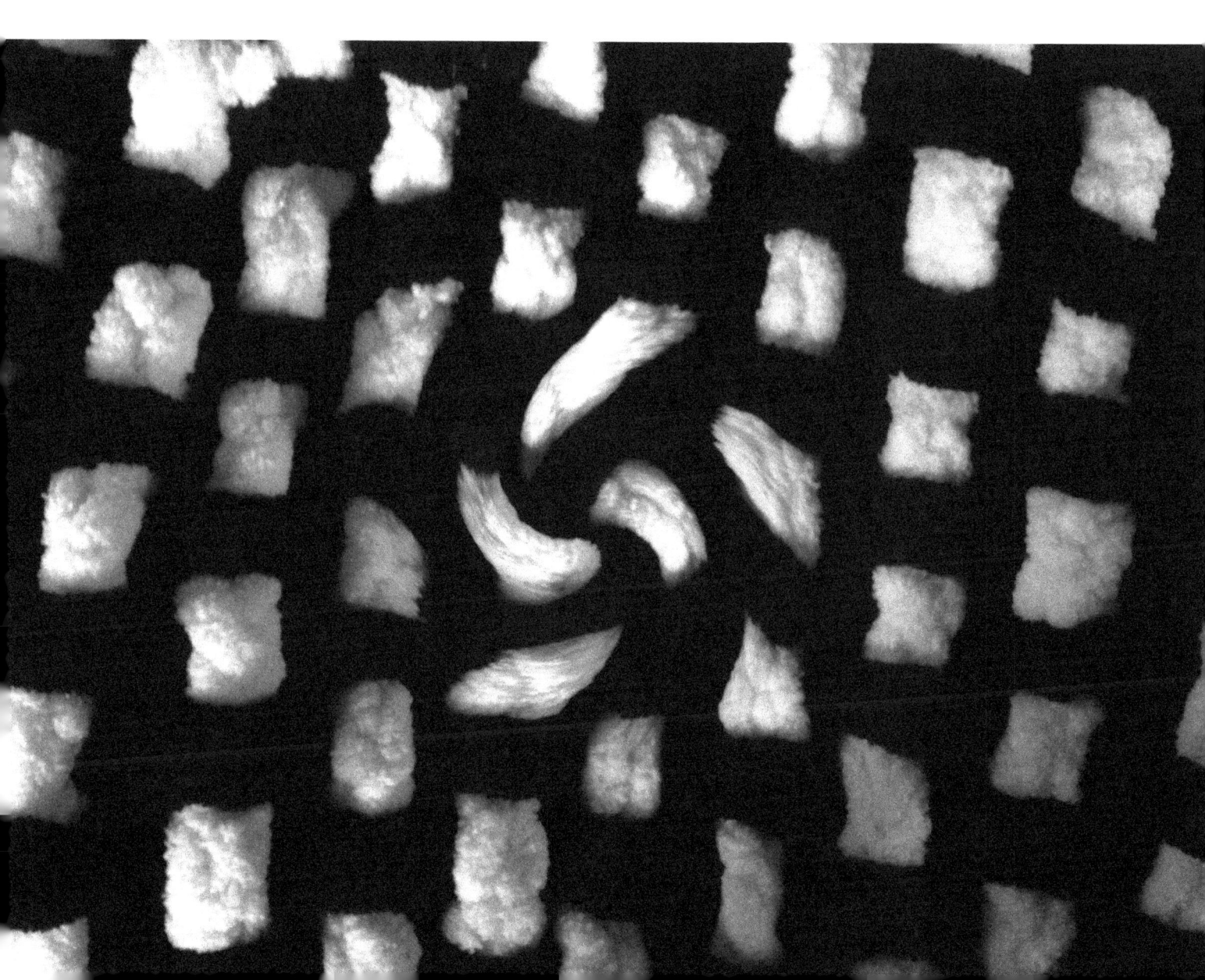

"Prepare yourself in every way you can by increasing your knowledge and adding to your experience, so that you can make the most of opportunity when it occurs."

Mario Andretti

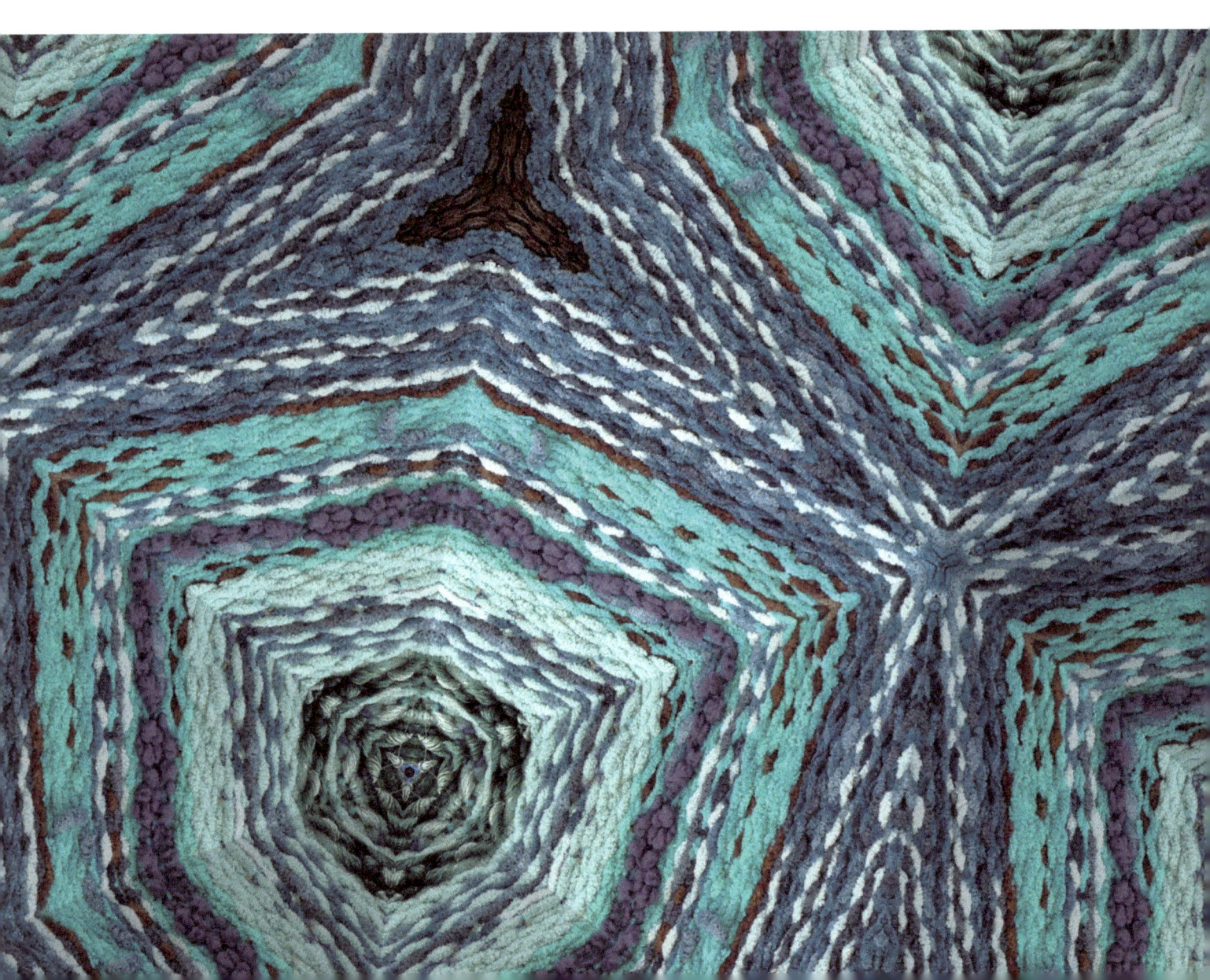

"We must remember that any oppression, any injustice, any hatred, is a wedge designed to attack our Civilization."

Franklin D. Roosevelt

"Every time I judge someone else, I reveal an unhealed part of myself."

Duperon

"Understand that the right to choose your own path is a sacred privilege. Use it. Dwell in possibility."

Oprah Winfrey

"With every experience, you and you alone are painting your own canvas, thought by thought, choice by choice."

Oprah Winfrey

"The highest form of human intelligence is to observe yourself without judgement."

Krishnamurti

Life as Art

Surrender

"The softest things in the world overcome the hardest things in the world. Through this I know the advantage of taking no action."

Lao - Tzu

Put the sword down and surrender to the reality that life, sometimes, is not fair. There is no need to pick up anything that is not yours. Now there's the rub, what belongs to you?

I hope, by this stage of our journey, you realize the choice is constantly in creation. We create our attitudes toward events. The facts remain the same, however, we do not.

It is a lovely paradox that judgements unexamined impede our growth and maturation. Our intent can be explored as we uncover the judgements.

Life as Art means there is no need to please another artist; no need to listen to who wants what and when. We are co-creators with the Devine and it is our human right to let others choose for themselves. No judgements, no insistence on right or wrong, good or bad, beautiful or ugly. "Now wouldn't it be a real drag if we were all the same." Savoy Brown

Of course the law informs us of societal imperatives and the consequent repercussions if we are in breach; but most of the time our intentions are noble, even if we are suffering.

At the point of surrender, "There's no need for arguments, there's no argument at all; And if you didn't hear from him it just means he didn't call." (Van Morrison, Domino)

"We must be willing to let go of the life we've planned, so as to have the life that is waiting for us".

Joseph Cambell

"The secret to change is to focus all of your energy, not on fighting the old, but on building the new."

Socrates

Compassion

"There is no King who has not had a Slave among his ancestors, and no Slave who has not had a King among his."

Helen Keller

Tara Brach states in her book, Radical Acceptance, that compassion is caring about caring. It is coming home to who we are. We all have the need to belong. Maslow said it is foundational toward self actualization.

In her Sounds True pod cast Tara spoke extensively to Rick Hanson about the notion of compassion as a direct response to suffering and our desire for connection.

Judgement and blame come from a place of hurt and/or fear. It is necessary to open your heart and examine where these feelings came from and forgive yourself for your transgression in order heal and forgive others.

This is the courageous journey toward compassion. Self love, peace and fearless examination of judgement, allows each us the chance to open our hearts and say,

"I'm sorry. I love you".

"There is something like a line of gold thread running through a man's words when he talks to his daughter, and gradually over the years it gets to be long enough for you to pick up in your hands and weave into a cloth that feel like love itself."

John Gregory Brown

"The purpose of human life is to serve and to show compassion and the will to help others."

Albert Schweitzer

"Whether we're a preschooler or a young teen, a graduating college senior or a retired person, we human beings all want to know that we're acceptable. That our being alive somehow makes a difference in the lives of others."

Fred Rogers

"It is not enough to begin; continuance is necessary. Mere enrolment will not make a scholar; the pupil must continue in the school through the long course, until he masters every branch. Success depends upon staying power. The reason for failure in most cases is lack of perseverance."

J.R. Miller

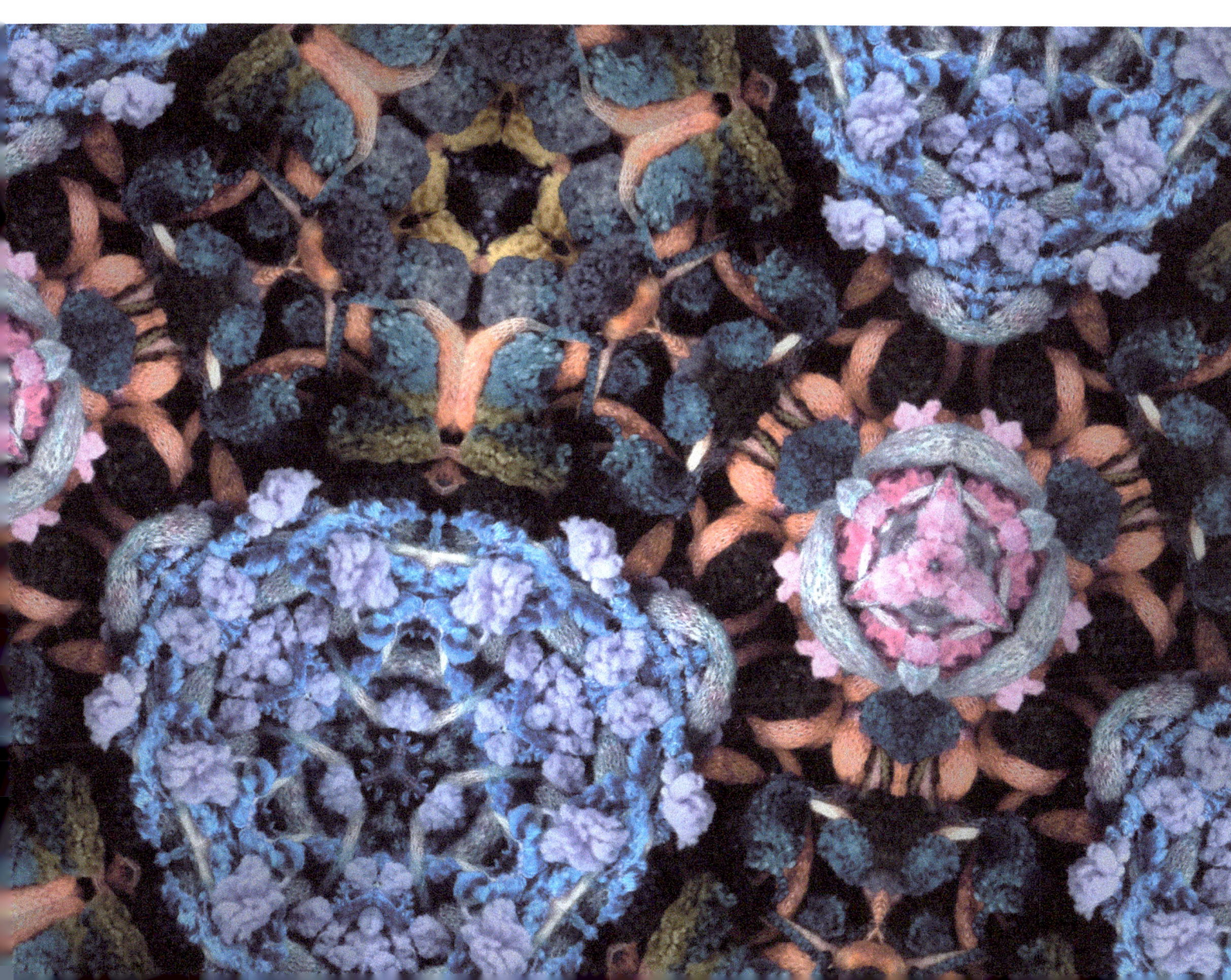

"Love yourself. Forgive yourself. How you treat yourself sets the standard for how others will treat you."

Dr. Steve Maraboli

"Owning our story and loving ourselves through that process is the bravest thing that we will ever do."

Dr. Brene Brown

"*I have come to believe that caring for myself is not self indulgent. Caring for myself is an act of survival.*"

Audre Lorde

"Your task is not to seek for love, but merely to seek and find all the barriers within yourself that you have built against it,"

Rumi

"When you react, you give away your power. When you respond, you are staying in control of yourself"

Bob Proctor

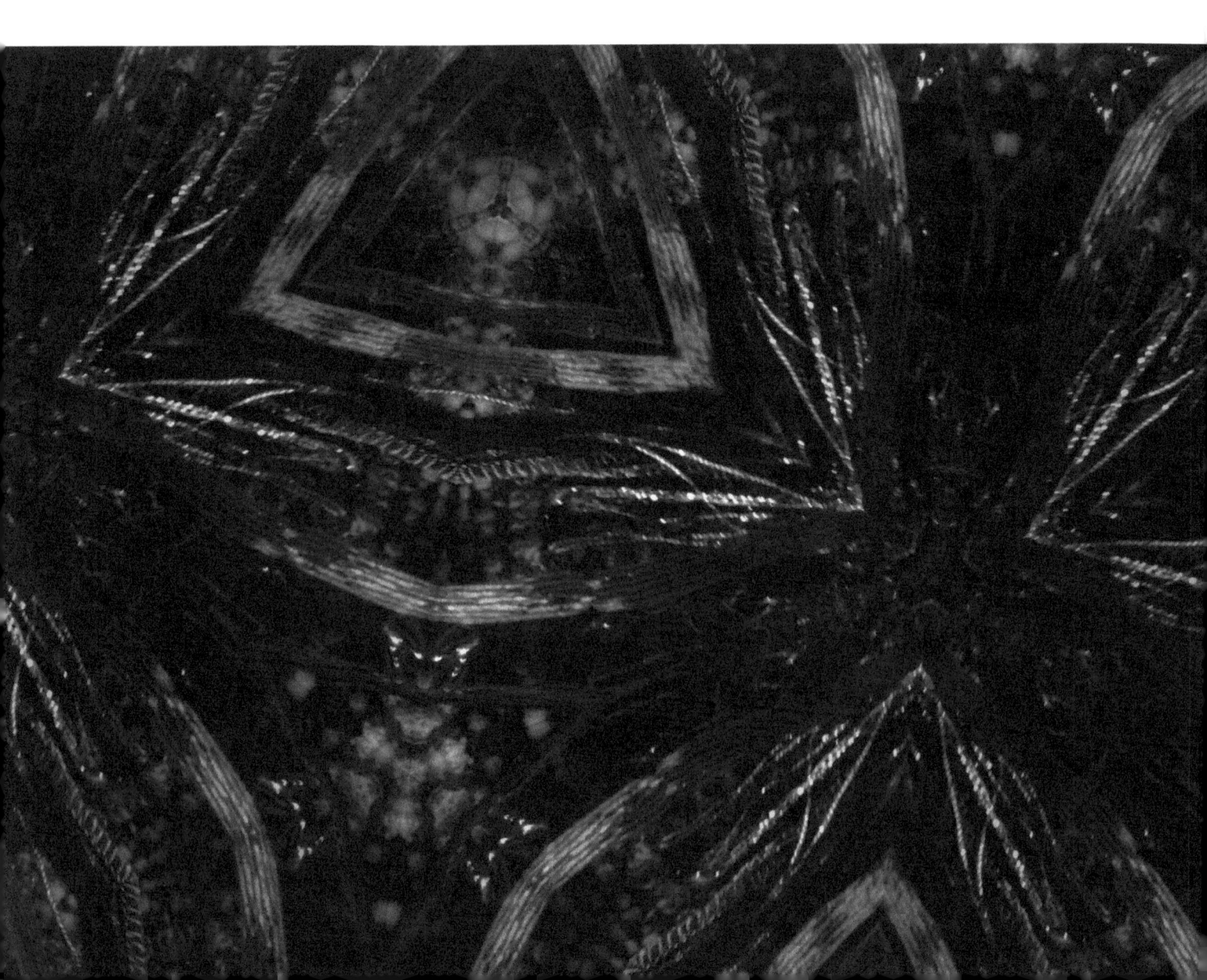

"Courage is what it takes to stand up and speak; courage is also what it takes to sit down and listen."

Winston Churchill

"One day at a time is all we should be dealing with. We can't go back to yesterday and we can't control tomorrow so we live today."

Lessons Learned in Life

Mindfulness is being aware of what's happening now without wishing it were different.
FACTS
Now go back from here

"Abstract is done by people who can't draw." Reply "I prefer inclusion to practiced exclusion." Conversation at Art Gallery.

About the Author

Gail Morningstar is a retired clinical therapist. She is presently an Integrative Life Coach in Yarmouth Nova Scotia. She uses Art, along with her skills as a registered Master Socialworker, to enhance her group participants requested change. She has studied for her Master of Socialwork at Wilfred Laurier University, Ontario Canada. University of Western Ontario BA Social Sciences (UWO) and Kings College UWO Thanatology and Palliative Care. She is also well versed in many esoteric fields including consciousness and a wide variety of subjects from many traditions.

CPSIA information can be obtained
at www.ICGtesting.com
Printed in the USA
BVHW021652250219
541084BV00020B/2100/P